Outdoor IQ

ULTIMATE

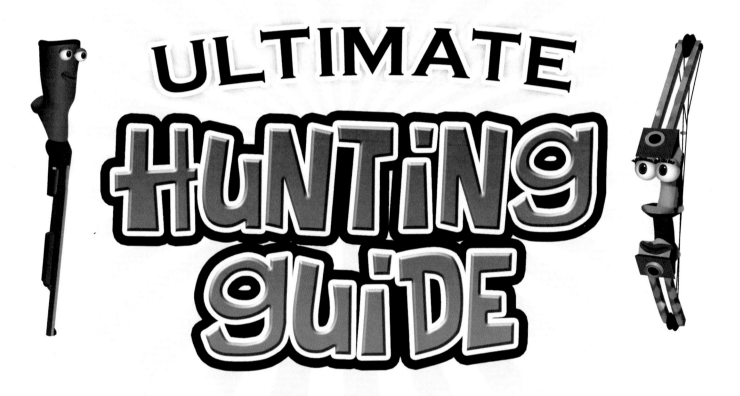

HUNTING GUIDE

JUST FOR KIDS!

BY DAVE AND STEVE SHELLHAAS

MIAMI VALLEY OUTDOOR MEDIA, LTD.

OutdoorIQ

For more information
address the publisher:
Miami Valley Outdoor Media, Ltd.
P.O. Box 35
Greenville, Ohio 45331

978-0-9845251-0-2
Printed and bound in USA.

Photographs by Steve and Dave
Shellhaas, and iStock photo stock

Disclaimer
All the Internet addresses (URLs) given
in this book were valid at the time
of going to press. However, due to
the dynamic nature of the Internet,
some addresses may have changed
or ceased to exist since publication.
While the authors and publisher regret
any inconvenience this may cause
readers, no responsibility for any such
changes can be accepted by either the
authors or the publisher.

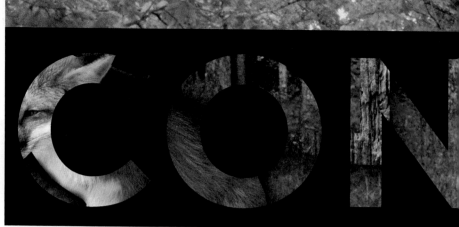

CON

TENTS

Ultimate Outdoor and Hunter Safety Tips

The Wild Turkey

Nicknames for Turkeys:

Jake: young male turkeys, usually 1-year-old

Tom, Long-beard or Gobbler: older male turkeys

Hens: female turkeys of any age

© iStockphoto/Stefan Ekernas

hen turkey

Habitat:

The wild turkey lives mostly in the woods. They like large trees, which provide a food source and provide safe roosting sites up off the ground.

In the spring the hen lays many eggs in a shallow nest on the ground.

photo courtesy of Marlin Stump

turkey nest

Differences between males and females:

Male turkeys have black feathers and very colorful heads. They weigh about 21 pounds.

Female turkeys have brown feathers and dull heads. They are smaller and weigh about 10 pounds.

What are beards and spurs!!

BEARDS

Males have what is known as a beard, a bristly mass of feathers found on the breast. Immature males, called jakes do not normally have an obvious beard. Bearded birds aren't always males. Sometimes you'll find a female with a beard.

A trophy turkey is a turkey with a very long beard, usually 10-12 inches!!

SPURS

Male turkeys have a claw on their legs above their back toe. These are called spurs. Spurs grow longer as the turkey gets older.

A trophy turkey is a turkey with very long spurs, usually 2 inches or more!!

beard

Food:

During the spring and summer, turkeys feed on insects, berries, green leaves and grass seeds. During the fall and winter, they feed more on acorns and fruits of trees like: oak, hop hornbeam, maple, ash, pine, and beech. Turkeys leave behind scratches on the ground where they have looked for food.

spurs

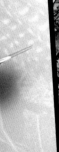

scratches

5

getting close to turkeys

TRICKS AND TIPS TO GET
CLOSE TO THOSE SMART BIRDS!!

How Do You Find Turkeys?

To find turkeys you have to look for clues that turkeys are in the area.

Clues can be turkey feathers on the ground. Turkeys sometimes lose a feather when they fly in and out of trees when they roost.

You can also look for turkey tracks. Turkeys sometimes leave tracks in wet dirt or sand.

What sounds do turkeys make?

Turkeys make many different sounds. By copying these sounds, you can bring the turkeys right to you!

The Yelp: A hen's call that says she is either happy, excited, or wants to invite a mate to come to her.

The Cluck: A hen turkey's call that says she is happy or excited.

The Gobble: The mating call of mature tom turkeys, used in the spring to attract hens.

The Purr: The purr is another happy call of the hen.

© iStockphoto/Stefan Ekernas

7

What is used to call turkeys to you?

There are all kinds of turkey calls that can help you get close to turkeys. The most common calls are box calls, slate calls, and diaphragm calls.

BOX CALLS

Box calls are the easiest to use. You slowly move the top of the box call across the top edge of the call to make the turkey sounds.

SLATE CALLS

Slate calls take a little practice. To make the sound you move the pencil-like striker across the surface of the slate. Moving it in different ways makes different sounds.

DIAPHRAGM CALLS

Diaphragm calls are put in your mouth. The half moon shaped call fits into the roof of your mouth. As you gently blow air out of your mouth, the call vibrates and makes a sound. With some practice you can make sounds just like a hen turkey!

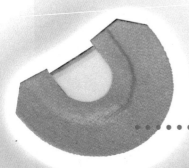

Real or not?

There are decoys that look like hens, some that look like jakes, and even tom turkey decoys in full strut. Full strut means that they have all of their feathers puffed out and their tail feathers spread to look their best for the hens.

A jake decoy makes the old toms jealous and can make them come in for a fight.

Give it a Try!

The next time you are out in the woods, either turkey hunting or just taking pictures, try some of these tips and see how close you can get to that big tom turkey!!

Hen decoys bring in the tom turkeys looking for a girlfriend.

Do it Yourself

The Cup Call
Turkey Call

sponge   cotton string   sharp pencil
empty yogurt cup   paper clip   camo tape
                  scissors

Step 2

Cut a piece of cotton string about 24 inches long.

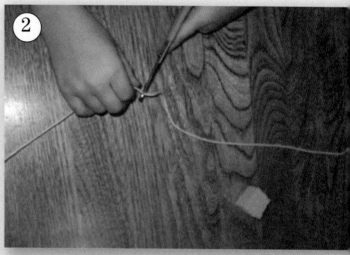

Step 1

Cut a rectangle that is 2 or 3 inches long from the sponge with your scissors. Be careful!! Have an adult help you if you have trouble.

Step 3

Have an adult poke a hole in the bottom of the cup with a sharp pencil.

Step 4

Put one end of the cotton string through the hole in the bottom of the cup. It may help to wet the end of the string so it goes through the hole easier.

Step 5

Tie a paper clip to string on the bottom side of the cup

Step 6

Tie the piece of sponge to the other end of the string.

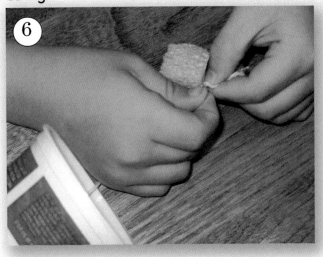

Step 7

Wrap a strip of camoflauge tape or fabric around the call.

How to Use the Call

1. Wet the sponge and wrap the sponge around the string up inside the cup.
2. Pull the sponge down the string to make a sound of a turkey.
3. Try different ways to make the call loud and soft.

11

TAKE A Turkey Hike

To stay healthy, you must get plenty of exercise and activity. A great way to get exercise this time of year is to take a "Turkey Hike". The wild turkey is common in most states and if you know there are turkeys in an area near you, a turkey hike can be a fun way to get outdoors and stay active.

This can also be a great way to scout an area you want to hunt for turkeys. As you hike through the woods, be on the look out for signs of turkeys. Here is what you can find:

Turkey Scratches
When turkeys are looking for food, they scratch the ground with their feet and claws. Where they claw up the ground is called a **scratch**.

You can find scratches in the woods or in a grassy field where turkeys are feeding.

scratch in the grass

scratch in the woods

tom track

hen track

turkey tracks

Turkey Tracks
If you find an area where it is wet or damp, you may find a turkey track. You can tell a tom track from a hen track because the tom's middle toe is very long.

Turkey Feathers
When turkeys fly down out of trees after they roost for the night, they sometimes lose a feather. Search the ground for these pretty feathers.

Turkey Nest
If you are really lucky and look carefully, you may even find a turkey nest full of eggs. Remember, do not disturb the eggs, the mother will soon return to keep her eggs warm.

Safety Note: Be sure to know when turkey season is open in your state before you take a turkey hike. It is not safe to walk in the woods if people are hunting turkeys, especially if you where red, blue and white colored clothing. Have fun but BE SAFE!!

Is Hunting Good or Bad??

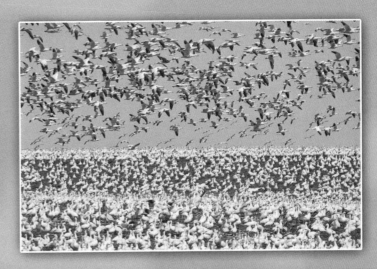

Reasons Hunting is Good for Wildlife

1 Hunting keeps populations of wildlife healthy. Without hunting, wildlife can become overpopulated (too many animals in a certain area) which can cause animals to starve or become sick from disease. Overpopulation of wildlife can also cause damage to the environment and property. Without hunting, the number of accidents from cars hitting wildlife would be much greater.

2 Money from hunting licenses pay for costs of wildlife management and protecting the habitat and open space in which the wildlife lives.

3 Money from hunting licenses helps to protect the environment and buy new areas of habitat that can be set aside for wildlife.

4 Money from hunting licenses also help to pay for reintroducing endangered animals that once lived in certain areas. Hunters and the money from their licenses have made it possible for the wild turkey to now be in every state except Alaska. Hunters and trappers have also helped to reintroduce river otters in many states. Without hunters and the money they spend, many animals may become even more endangered or even extinct.

Many people and groups try to make people believe hunting is cruel and harmful to wildlife. That is NOT TRUE! As you see, hunters are responsible for protecting the environment, increasing habitat, keeping animal populations healthy and reintroducing and protecting endangered wildlife.

HUNTING IS VERY IMPORTANT TO ALL WILDLIFE!!!

The Groundhog
(Marmota monax)

Groundhog Fun Facts

- Also called Woodchucks or Whistle pigs.
- Largest members of the squirrel family.
- Hibernate like bears during the winter.
- Communicate with a loud whistle sound.
- Have short, powerful legs for digging.
- Their two front teeth never stop growing, must be worn down by chewing.

What is a trophy size 'Hog?

- Grow up to 2 foot tall.
- Weigh up to 13 pounds.
- Tail grows up to 10 inches in length.
- Males grow larger than females.

Pacific Ocean

Atlantic Ocean

Where do they live?

Groundhogs are found in eastern and central United States, northward across Canada and into Alaska.

Where they live:

• Where woods meet open areas, like farm fields, streams, and roads.
• Live underground in dens, digging tunnels that can be up to 30 feet long, and have up to 5 exit holes.
• Groundhogs can remove over 700 pounds of dirt to make their tunnels.
• The tunnels can be as deep as 5 feet under ground.

What they eat:

• Groundhogs are herbivores. This means they eat a variety of plants including dandelion, clover, peas, beans, grasses, grains, fruits, and tree bark.

• A groundhog can eat 1/3 of their body weight in food each day.

• Sometimes they will eat insects, snails, and birds' eggs but it is uncommon.

Groundhogs are cool!

Groundblinds for Groundhogs
BASIC TRAINING FOR DEER HUNTING

Hunting groundhogs is a great way that you can learn and practice the skills you will need to be a good deer hunter. This "basic training" will teach you skills like finding sign, figuring out how fresh the sign is, scouting using trail cameras, using food to increase your odds, and setting up and hunting from a blind. Now use these steps to hunt groundhogs and also become a skilled deer hunter!

Step ① Find the Holes

• Walk the edges of fence rows, streams, and woods.

• In crop fields, look for areas that have been eaten (may look lighter or plants are smaller).

• Look by stumps, rock piles, or by old buildings.

Step ② Make sure hole is fresh

• Look for fresh dirt that was pushed out of hole.

• Look for plants that have been eaten or stems and leaves that have been bitten off.

• Check for other holes around the main entrance.

16

Step ③ Scout the Groundhog
(or Patterning the Groundhog)

- Use a trail camera to know when the groundhog is leaving the hole.

- Place the camera on a tree, stake, or metal rod. Place camera 2-3 feet from hole and aim it at the opening.

- After a few days, take the camera or the memory card home to see cool pictures and plan the best time to hunt the groundhog.

Trail camera will print date and time the picture was taken. This helps pattern the groundhog and know when it is active.

27Jul2007 08:14

Step ④ Bait the Groundhog

- To increase your chances of seeing groundhogs, you can bait the hole.

- Use carrots, lettuce, apples, or other veggies. **Apples are their favorite!!!**

- Place apples and veggies 2-3 feet from the hole, but make sure to stake them down with metal rods.

- This keeps the groundhog from pulling the apples or veggies back into its hole.

17

Step ⑤ Setting the Blind

• Use a ground blind with chairs or stools inside.

• Set up the blind about 15-20 yards from the hole you have been baiting.

• Place the blind behind hole or to the side of hole. Never have the blind facing the hole.

• Be quiet, set up quickly, and wait.

• The best time to hunt is early morning or dusk. Remember to use the trail camera to find out when the groundhog is active . . .

Step ⑥ Hunting from the Blind

• Keep all windows in the blind shut except for the one facing the hole.

• Make sure the ground is clear of leaves and sticks to help keep noise down.

• Have your camera or gun ready and wait for the groundhog to come out of its hole!!

• Be sure to always hunt with a grown up and follow all hunter safety rules!!

Tips for Groundblind Success

No matter if you are hunting ground-hogs, deer or turkey, groundblinds are a great way to get close to animals. Groundblinds are also great for kids because they do not have to stay still the whole time while hunting.

Here are some tips that will help you be more successful hunting from ground-blinds.

What to Wear

• Since you usually sit in a chair or on a stool, it doesn't really matter what you wear for pants.

• However, it is important to wear a black shirt or jacket, black gloves and even a black facemask or covering over your head.

• Most ground blinds have a black lining inside. To blend with the inside of the blind, you need to wear black, NOT camo or light clothes.

• Look at the pictures and see how much difference wearing black makes.

Have Something to Do

• No matter what you are hunting for, you may have to wait a while. To make the wait go faster, take something to do in the blind.
• The blind is a great place to get your homework done. You can quietly write in your notebook or just draw pictures of what you see outside.
• You can also take your OutdoorIQ magazine or other books to read in the blind!!
• If you just can't leave your video game at home, you can even bring it along. BE SURE THE SOUND IS TURNED OFF!!!
• No matter what you do to pass the time, be sure to be alert and make sure you are ready for that important shot when the time comes!!! Good luck!!!

The Basics of Using a Trail Camera

Trail cameras can be very important gear for hunters. These cameras can be used to find out what animals are in the area you want to hunt. The cameras take a picture when an animal walks in front of the camera. You can place trail cameras at the edge of a field, near a feeder or on a trail the animals are using.

Although there are all brands and kinds of trail cameras, there are some basics you can learn to help you be successful. This article will show you the basics of how to set up and use trail cameras so you can scout the animals you want to hunt.

Setting up the Camera

All trail camera use batteries of some kind. Many trail cameras use "D" cell batteries. So the first thing you need to do is put batteries in your camera.

The second thing you need to do is put in a memory card in the camera. Most cameras use a memory card called an "SD card". The SD cards come in different memory sizes like 128 MB or 2 GB. Have an adult help you decide what size card is best. The more memory the card has, the more pictures it will hold.

Using the Camera in the Field

After you have the batteries and memory card in the camera, it is ready to be set up out in the field. Find the place you want to put your camera. You can put it on a tree near a trail or even on a post near a hole, like we did in the groundhog article.

After you place the camera where you want it, follow the instructions that came with your camera to make sure the camera is ready to take pictures and is turned on.

Checking the Camera for Pictures

After a few days, go out and check the camera. Most cameras have a screen that tells you how many pictures have been taken. If you have several pictures, take the memory card out and replace it with another one if you do not want to miss taking any pictures.

You can then take the card home and have an adult help you view the pictures on a computer. Many printers and computers have card readers that will read the pictures on the card and download them to the computer.

Download the pictures to see what great pictures your trail camera captured!!

Checking out the Picture

Most trail cameras have a feature that puts the date and time on the picture. This helps you know when the animal was active and there in front of your camera.

You can use that information to know what time is best to out in the field to see the animal. If most of the pictures are taken at a certain time, you better be there around that time if you want to see the animal for yourself!!

Trail cameras are fun to use. You can now use what you learned to set up and use a trail camera of your own. You can find trail cameras at most sporting goods stores and department stores. Trail cameras range from around $ 50 up to $ 500. Start out with an inexpensive, easy to use camera. There are many good beginner cameras for $ 50 - $ 100.

Get out there and see what surprises you find on your trail camera pictures!!!

The Crow

©istockphoto/Stephen Muskie

Quick Crow Facts

- Crows are found all around the world except New Zealand, South America and Antarctica.
- The American or Common crow is the most common crow in North America.
- Both male and female crows have black feathers, bills, legs, feet and claws.
- The crow's weight averages about a pound with a body length from 15" to 21" and a wingspan up to 36".
- Crows can fly 30 mph with short bursts as fast as 60 mph.
- Crow's eyesight is very good and is similar to a wild turkey.

©istockphoto/Alexander Chelmodeev

Where Crows Live

Crows live in many habitats. They use woodlands for roosting, nesting and perching. They can be also found in open areas, agricultural fields, coastal wetlands, marshes, rivers and streams looking for food.

What Crows Eat

Crows are omnivores, this means they eat plants and animals. Their diet consists of almost anything: seeds, fruits, nuts, insects, mollusks, earthworms, eggs, nestlings, frogs, mice, garbage and carrion (dead animal meat). They are attracted to garbage dumps and they also like melons and corn. Farmers placing scarecrows in their fields was caused by the crow's eating and damaging crops. Crows do help farmers, however, when they eat insects attracted by their crops.

Enemies

Crow's natural enemies are owls, usually the great horned and some of the larger hawks (red-tailed, red-shouldered and goshawks). To protect themselves, they will often gang-up on or "mob" an enemy until it leaves the area. Man is the number one enemy of the crow.

Living Together

Crows are very social and live in family groups of between 2 to 15 birds. Crows are territorial and protect their territory very well. They have roosts where they gather just before dark after returning from feeding on normal flight paths called flyways. When roosts are located in towns, they cause many problems especially when there are thousands of birds. Towns have fought them with firecrackers, propane cannons, repellents and, sometimes, chain saws.

A Smart Bird

The crow is probably the most intelligent bird in North America. Crows quickly learn that a moving car is no danger, but will rapidly flee if the driver stops and gets out. In areas where they are constantly hunted, they learn the difference between a hunter with a gun and a farmer with farming implements.

Pet crows are known to have an unusual ability to imitate the sounds of the human voice. They can learn simple words like "mama," "papa," "hello," "howdydo," and others. The sounds of human laughter are often imitated to perfection.

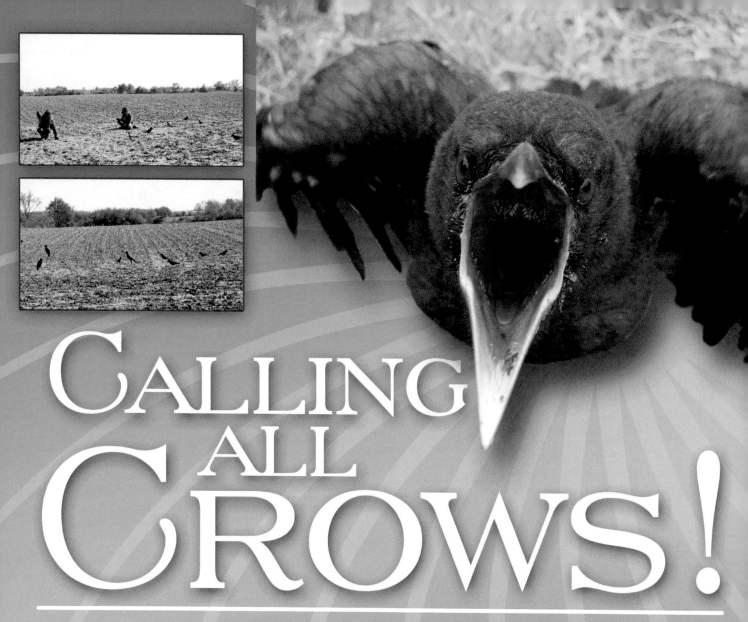

CALLING ALL CROWS!

THE BASICS OF CROW HUNTING

If you want some fast, fun action, try your hand at hunting crows. Crows are found in all areas of the U.S. and Canada and can be casily called into range for the young hunter. Because the action is fast and exciting, young hunters find this activity a "blast"!

Finding Crows

Before you can shoot crows, you must find them. It may seem like crows are everywhere, and in fact, it is possible to call in and shoot a few crows just about anywhere.

Pre-hunt scouting can really improve your luck. Fortunately for us, crows are very noisy and easily seen. Keep an eye on newly cut fields for feeding crows.

The farmers usually dislike the crow and will usually give you permission to hunt crows. As always, conduct yourself in a courteous and respectful way.

Gearing Up
Crow hunting does not require a lot of expensive gear.

Choose a Gun and Shot

The beginning crow hunter needs a good shotgun that the hunter is comfortable shooting. Although any gauge shotgun can be used. If the young hunter is comfortable shooting a 20 gauge or even a 12 gauge, the chances of success are much better. As far as shot size, #6 shot seems to be crow hunters favorite but #7 1/2 and #8 shot will also work.

Calls

There are basically two types of crow calls, electronic and hand. Each have a place in crow calling and very often they can be used together.

Hand calls are the cheaper of the two and easy to carry. Most are made of plastic or some hardwood and utilize a plastic or metal reed. When picking a hand call there are some features to be considered. Try to find a call that is easy to blow. Crow hunting requires long calling with a lot of volume. A hard to blow call will wear you out in a hurry.

Electronic callers can produce the sounds of many crows at the same time, something that is hard to do with a single hand call. There are now cassette and CD callers or the digital callers. All use rechargeable batteries and can produce loud calls.

Beginning crow hunters can have quick, fun results with these units right off the shelf. Callers that produce good volume and clear sound are the best units for crow calling.

To hear examples of the different types of calls crows make, go to http://www.crowbusters.com/begtechn_dc.htm.

Hand Call

Electronic Cassette Caller

Electronic Digital Caller

Camouflage

Crows have great eyesight and can see movement from a long way off, and can also see color. It is very important that you be camouflaged as completely as possible, including gloves and a face mask. Pick a pattern that best matches the surroundings. Also, don't forget to check your gun for any flashy surfaces that might give you away.

Decoys

Besides calling, the best thing you can do to increase your success at attracting crows is to use decoys.

Types of Decoys

There are two kinds of decoys, silhouette and full bodied. Both types will attract crows, but each has advantages and disadvantages.

The silhouette decoy is just a flat, black cut out of a crow. You can make them at home by tracing the outline of a crow on cardboard or thin plywood, cutting them out, and then spray painting with a solid coat of flat black. (See page 28 for directions on how to make your own)

Full bodied decoys look the most real and are easy to set up. However, they cost more and are harder to carry. If you want to set up a crow vs. owl scene, you will also need an owl decoy. Most owl decoys you buy look like the Great Horned Owl and are made of hard plastic. You can find these at the local garden store.

Friendly Decoy Set Up >>

The Friendly setup looks like a group of feeding crows. Use this set up where you see crows, usually in a field, orchard or dump. Put a few decoys up as high as you can in the trees to let crows to see the decoys from far away. DO NOT put decoys around your blind. This will let them see you easier.

<< Fighting Set Up

The Fighting setup is where the crows are fighting with something, like a an owl or hawk, or even other crows. The best set up is to put an owl decoy so that every crow in the area can spot it. A fence post, the top of a small tree, or even on a tall pole works great. Put most of your decoys in the trees and brush around the owl decoy.

Another Fun Way to Crow Hunt

The Hopscotch Method

The Hopscotch or Hit and Run method is a fun way to hunt crows and can be used even in an area that you are not familiar with. Hunters look for small groups of feeding or calling crows. You find a good place to hide or make a blind and start calling. Usually, at least a few crows will come to your calls.

*SAFETY NOTE:
Always be sure to obey all local hunting regulations and gun safety practices when crow hunting. Crows are also known to carry the West Nile virus that can infect humans. Try not to touch the blood of the crow and always wash your hands after touching the crows in any way.

>>> You can have fun making your own crow decoys that **REALLY WORK!!** Here is what you do:

Step 1
- Trace the outline of the crow on this page onto another piece of paper.
- You can also find the outline of the crow at our website and print it off. Go to: http://www.outdoorkidsclub.com/diy.html

Step 2
- Cut out the outline you traced or printed off and trace it onto a piece of thick cardboard or plywood. You should make it bigger if you are able to.

Step 3
- Have a grown up help you cut out the cardboard or plywood crow shape.

Step 4
- Paint the cut out black on both sides.

Step 5
- Glue a clothes pin or wooden dowel rod to the cut out. HINT: Hot glue works best, but have a grown up help you.

Step 6
- Use the clothes pin to clip the decoy to a branch or stick the dowel in the ground.
- Have fun using your decoys to bring in crows!

The Habitat Connection

Food Chains and Food Webs

A big part of any habitat are the food chains and food webs that you find in that habitat. If the food chains or webs are changed or damaged, the animals in that habitat can be in danger.

So what are food chains and food webs?

Food Chain

A **food chain** is a simple group of living things that rely on each other for food. A food chain can be made up of three or more living things.

Most food chains begin with some type of plant. Plants take energy from the sun to help them live and grow. Other animals then eat the plants for their energy. Another animal can eat that animal, and that makes a food chain.

An example of a woodland food chain is acorns that are eaten by a squirrel that is then eaten by a fox.

Coyotes eat the turkeys, squirrels and foxes.

Turkeys eat the acorns.

A fox eats the squirrel.

Oak Tree produces acorns.

Squirrels eat the acorns.

A foxhawk eats the squirrel.

Food Web

A **food web** is really just many food chains that connect together. In a food web, there can be different animals sharing certain plants or animals for food.

In our woodland example, turkeys also eat acorns and hawks also eat squirrels. We can also add coyotes that eat turkeys, squirrels and even foxes. That makes up a food web.

Healthy Habitats

A healthy habitat has several food chains and food webs. If plants or animals are lost from a habitat it makes a break in a food chain. This break can cause the other animals that use that plant or animal for food to die. It is important that we do our part to keep habitats healthy.

Responsible hunting and fishing help to keep the populations of animals in check so that all food chains and food webs stay in place. Try to think of a food chain or food web around you.

Squirrels

365 species of Squirrels

Consist of:
Tree Squirrels
Ground Squirrels
Flying Squirrels

• Squirrels are found everywhere in the world except for Australia and the Antarctica.
• In the US, there are about 10 types of Tree Squirrels.
• Gray squirrels, Fox squirrels and Red squirrels are the most common squirrels in the United States.

Black colored squirrel

Albino squirrel

Grey squirrel

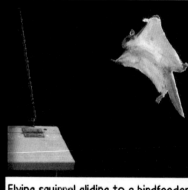

Flying squirrel gliding to a birdfeeder

A squirrel's teeth grow all the time, up to 6 inches a year. They must keep chewing on nuts, seeds, or branches to keep them the right size.

Squirrels' brains are the size of a walnut.

They can fall 100 feet from a tree and not hurt themselves.

Their long bushy tails are used for balance, an umbrella from rain/sun, warmth, and to communicate with other squirrels.

A Squirrel's Diet

Nuts, seeds, fruit, bugs, mushrooms, bird eggs, and flowers.

Squirrels have to eat about 1 pound of food per week to keep active.

They live in trees, holes in the trunk or in treetop nests called Dreys. These nests can be made of leaves, twigs, and moss.

Fox squirrel

A squirrel will lick or rub a nut on its face before it will bury the nut. This allows the squirrel to find the nut later by searching for that scent.

They can find these buried nuts even through a foot of snow.

Nutty Fact: A single squirrel can hide 10,000 nuts each year.
The squirrel will not find every nut, and the nuts not found will turn into new trees.

Red squirrel

The adult male squirrel is the cleanest member of the Rodent family.

Squirrels are most active in the first few hours after sunrise, and the last few hours before sunset.

Squirrel Dogs

A FUN WAY TO HUNT SQUIRRELS

Squirrel hunting is a fun activity but sometimes waiting quietly for the squirrels to appear can be hard. If waiting quietly or sneaking quietly through the woods in search of squirrels is not easy for you, try using squirrel dogs!!

What exactly are squirrel dogs?

Squirrel dogs are special dogs trained to smell out squirrels and track them to a tree. There are many types of dogs that can be trained to be squirrel dogs. Two breeds of dogs that make excellent squirrel dogs include the feist and the cur breeds.

How do you hunt with squirrel dogs?

Squirrel hunting with dogs is nonstop action!! You let the dogs loose in the woods and they go and find the trail of a squirrel and track them to a tree. You follow the dogs or listen for their barking and then go find where the dogs have treed a squirrel. If you have ever hunted for raccoons with dogs, this is exactly the same. The only difference is that you can do this during the day.

Here the trail has led to the bottom of this tree.

The dogs have a squirrel treed.

33

What happens once the dogs tree a squirrel?

Once you find the dogs at the tree where they have treed the squirrel, you look up and try to find the squirrel in the branches above. Look close, sometimes they will be way at the top of the tree. Sometimes they will jump from branch to branch trying to get away from the dogs. Be sure to follow them before they get away.

Sometimes, you may even find a raccoon in the tree instead of a squirrel. If it is raccoon season, that may be a bonus to your hunt!

©istockphoto/Peter Blanchard

What gun is best for squirrel hunting with dogs?

As always, you should use a gun that you are comfortable shooting. The gun should be light enough that you can safely carry it through the woods as you follow the dogs from tree to tree. It is also important that you are comfortable shooting high above your head because that is where many of the squirrels will be.

You can use either a shotgun or a .22 rifle for this type of squirrel hunting. Remember, the squirrels may be jumping from limb to limb, so a shotgun might be the best to use for those situations. However, if you are a really good shot with a .22 rifle, using that gun can be a fun challenge too!!

The Results of the Hunt!!

If you find a place with a lot of squirrels and you have some good squirrel dogs, you should have a fun and successful hunt. Make sure you practice with your gun so you are ready when you get that important shot at the squirrel. If you make a good shot, the squirrel will fall and one of the dogs will go find it and bring it to you.

Here is the OutdoorIQ Gang and Luke Drew at the end of a pretty good afternoon of squirrel hunting with dogs!

Safety Tips

- Always be sure you hunt with a grown up and be sure of the background where you are shooting.
- NEVER RUN after the dogs while carrying your gun.
- It is best to load your gun once the dogs have treed the squirrel and you are under the tree and see the squirrel.
- Always know where the other hunters and the dogs are before you shoot.

Whitetail Deer

(Odocoileus virginianus)

Whitetail Facts:

Grayish-brown color in fall/winter
Reddish-brown color in spring/summer

White areas on neck, eyes, nose, belly, and underneath side of tail

Can run 30-40 mph, jump 8-9 feet, and can swim well.

Males weigh 150-300 pounds
Females weigh 90-200 pounds

Smallest Member of the Deer family

Deer's Diet:

Deer eat tree leaves, grass, berries, acorns, herbs, twigs, corns, alfalfa, and fruits.

Deer feed more at dawn and dusk.

Whitetails are found in most of U.S., except for southwest, Alaska, and Hawaii. They are also found in Southern Canada.

A group of deer is called a **herd**.

A Male deer is called a Buck

Bucks grow a new set of antlers every year.

Antlers start growing in spring and finish growing by September. As the antlers grow they are covered by a fuzzy skin called **velvet**. The velvet is rubbed off in the fall after the antlers become hard. The antlers will fall off in late winter.

Bucks use their antlers to rub trees and fight other bucks during the "Rut".

A female deer is called a Doe

Does give birth to 1, 2, or 3 babies in May or June, they are called **fawns**.

A fawn is usually reddish in color with small white spots. These spots help hide and camouflage the fawn in the wild.

They will loose these spots in the winter when they are 5-7 months old.

Did you know??

The whitetail is the most popular large game animal in the U.S.

Deer have good eyesight and hearing, but their sense of smell is the best.

Deer have special stomachs that have 4 chambers. This allows them to digest some plants and foods that other animals can't.

37

The Sounds Deer Make

Learning the sounds that deer make can help you be a better deer hunter. Knowing what sounds deer make and why they make them can help you see more deer when you are out hunting.

> Doe Sounds

Doe calls can be useful in calling in does and even bucks sometimes. Does make several sounds for different reasons.

Contact Call

This is a sound a does makes when she is trying to locate other deer in her family. This sound is a soft humming or long bleating sound.

You can try to copy this sound to get deer to come closer to see what deer is lost. Use a bleat call and make two to three long, loud bleats.

Doe Grunt

When a deer grunts, it is saying "Hey, come over here". Doe grunts are soft and not very loud. If the grunt is too loud, it makes the deer become alerted and looking for danger.

Using a grunt call that makes doe grunts, you can make one to three very soft grunts. Be sure to wait a little between each grunt. If nothing happens, try it again in 15 to 20 minutes.

Doe Bleat

When a doe bleats, it is telling other deer, "Hey, I am over here". This sound is used by does to keep their fawns close by. This sound is a very soft, short bleating sound.

Using a call that makes bleat calls, make one to three soft, short bleats. This may draw a doe to you or even bring in a buck that thinks a doe is in the area.

Alarm Snort

This is the sound does and bucks make when they sense danger. They snort and blow air out their nose making a loud blowing or snorting sound. This sound tells other deer there is something wrong or danger is near.

This is a call you do not want to hear when you are hunting. Many times deer make this sound if they smell you but do not see you. They will usually run away shortly after making the snort.

> Buck Sounds

Buck calls and sounds are different than doe calls. Bucks make sounds for different reasons than the does make their sounds. The buck's sounds are made mostly during the rut or the deer's breeding season. Copying these sounds can make for an exciting hunt if a buck hears your calls.

Buck Grunt

A buck makes a grunt for the same reason a doe makes a grunt. It is to tell another deer to "come here". The main difference is that a buck grunt is much lower or deeper than the doe grunt. The older and bigger the buck, the deeper the grunt is.

You can use a deer grunt call to make a buck grunt and get a buck to come and see what deer is calling. Just be sure not to make a too deep of grunt or that may scare away small or younger bucks!

Tending Grunt

This is a grunt sound that bucks make when they are following a doe during the rut. When bucks make the tending grunt, he is trying to get her to stop.

To make this call, you make several, soft, short grunts right after one another. This can be a really good call if you are on the ground hunting and walking through the leaves. A buck may hear that and come to see where this strange buck is walking or trailing a doe.

Sparring sounds

These are sounds of two bucks calmly pushing each other around by their antlers. This sound is common in the early season when bucks are living together in groups.

This sound can be made using rattling antlers, real antlers or rattle bags. To copy sparring sounds, it is important to slowly rattle the antlers together or slowly roll the rattle bag between your hands. This is NOT a buck fight and is not a real loud, crashing antler sound.

> Sounds bucks make when they are MAD!!!

There are two sounds that bucks make when they are really mad and upset. These sounds are usually made in the middle of the rutting season.

Snort-Wheeze

This is not a very common sound but bucks do make it when they meet another buck in their area. They make a loud snort sound and then a wheezing sound by blowing air out of their nose.

This call can really scare smaller, younger bucks. If they hear this sound they usually take off running. If two big bucks meet up and they snort-wheeze at each other, a fight may be next.

Aggressive Rattling

This sound is made when those to big bucks start fighting. When bucks fight, they crash their antlers into the other buck's antlers making a loud rattling sound.

You can make this sound by crashing real or rattling antlers together very hard and loud. Remember, you are trying to make it sound like two bucks are really going at it. When a buck hears two bucks fighting in his area, he will quickly come to see who is fighting in the area and try to chase them away.

© istock/ Paul Tessier

40

Tips to Calling Deer

Calling deer is not magic and will not work everytime. However, deer calls and rattling can work at certain times of the year and help you see more deer. Here are some tips to remember when you are trying to call in deer.

• Learn what the different deer sounds sound like. Listen to recordings of deer sounds or calls. You can hear the deer calls mentioned in this article on our website under the News and Updates page. Click on Deer Calls on that page to find the deer call sounds or go to www.outdoorkidsclub.com/deercalls

• Do not call too often. Deer do not make sounds all the time. If you are calling too much, the deer will figure out the sound is probably not coming from another deer. Only call every 15 to 20 minutes.

• Keep the deer from smelling you before they see you. Try to stay down wind (keep the wind blowing from the deer to you) when you call so they do not smell you. Stay clean and try to keep your "human" smell down as best as you can and use deer scent to cover your scent and fool the deer's nose.

• Practice, practice, practice. Practice making the sounds with your deer call and rattling antlers or rattle bag. The more you practice, the more you will sound like a real deer and the better your chances of calling the deer to you.

• Be safe. Because you are copying the sounds real deer make, you must be ready for deer to react and come to you. If you call on the ground, you must be alert and hunt with a grown up. Calling bucks in with calls or rattling antlers during the rut can be dangerous, so BE VERY CAREFUL!!!

There are many different calls that you can buy. Here are a few of the different types of calls that you can buy.

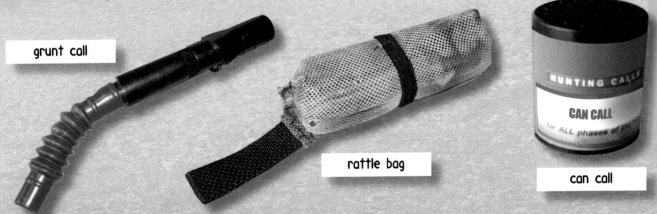

grunt call

rattle bag

can call

Calling deer can be very exciting and a great way of getting deer to come closer to you. Use what you have learned in this article and practice the different calls and sounds and see how close you can get deer to come to you. Just remember, always have a grown up with you and stay safe.

Rattle Bags

Materials Needed

- package of small **square** dowels
- single thin black sock
- small rope or twine
- thick rubber band

Tools:
- Hacksaw
- Scissors

1 Have an adult cut square dowel to 6 inch pieces.

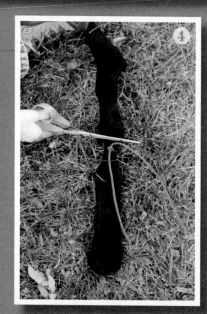

2 Place 10 dowels into the black sock.

3 Tie a piece of small rope about 1-2 inches above the end of the dowels. Leave the end of the rope long.

4 Cut off extra part of sock above the rope.

5 Tie large rubber band onto long part of the rope.

6 The rubber band goes around the dowels to keep it together and quiet when rattle bag is not in use.

How to use a Rattle Bag

Slap the bag loudly between your hands.

Roll the bag back and forth between your hands. This can be done fast or slow.

To sound like two bucks fighting, begin by slapping the bag first. Then roll the bag fast and slow, it can also be soft and loud. Slapping in between rolling bag can also be done. Just have fun.

BE A DEER DETECTIVE

If you deer hunt, this is an important time of year. For some states, deer season has already started. For others, the season is right around the corner. No matter if the season has started or will not start for another month, this is the time to get out in the woods and fields and find clues that deer are in the area you want to hunt!!

Here are some ways you can scout and find clues so you can see more deer when you are hunting!!

deer feeding in a soybean field

Find the Food
Deer have to eat. If can find what they are eating, you can figure out where they are. Deer eat different food at different times of the year.

In farming areas at this time of year, the food is soybeans and corn. Look around these areas in the morning and evening to find deer. Good clues to look for in these areas are eaten bean leaves and ears of corn nibbled while it is still on the stalk.

acorns

In the forests, find oak trees. Deer love to eat the acorns that fall from the oak trees. Look for the white oak trees. They are the first to drop their acorns. Good clues are acorns cracked in half with the inside gone.

Look for tracks
This may seem simple and sometimes it is. If you find tracks, you know the deer has been there. Tracks can tell you where a deer is traveling. However, tracks are hard to find if the ground is hard or the ground is covered with leaves. You will have to look hard to find clues there.

very good deer trail entering a field

deer trail in the forest

Look for places there are new tracks and old tracks. If you find this, the deer are using this trail very often.

Also pay attention to trails and the direction the tracks are going. This can tell you where the deer are coming from and where they are going.

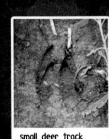
large deer track

small deer track

Track tip: It is very hard to tell much about the deer from its track. Buck and doe tracks look very similar. The size of the track sometimes be a clue to how big the deer is but not always.

SCOUTING FOR CLUES LEFT BY DEER

As the season goes on, the bucks will leave new clues that they are using a certain area. If you find these clues, you know a big buck may be close by!!

large tree rubbed with paw marks

Nice Rub!

small rubs from shedding velvet

small rub

Rubs

Rubs are named for how these are made. They are places where the bucks "rub" the bark off of trees. They do this for two reasons.

Reason 1:
Early in the fall, bucks have to get the velvet (the skin that covers the antlers when they are growing) off of their antlers. To do this, they rub their antlers on trees. Bucks usually use small trees to do this.

Reason 2:
Later in the season, bucks are getting ready for the rut (the deer's mating season). At this time, bucks begin to rub their antlers on larger trees to make their necks stronger in case they have to fight another buck. They also make rubs as a sign to other bucks saying "I was here".

Rub scouting tip:
The size of rubs can sometimes tell you how big the buck may be. Big and small bucks both rub small trees. However, small bucks do not often rub large trees. If you find a rub on a big tree (3 inches in diameter or more), you know there is a big buck in the area!!

Scrapes

Scrapes are made when a buck "scrapes" the leaves and other stuff on the ground away to get down to the soil. Scrapes are made by the bucks to attract does and let other bucks know they are in the area.

Smell is Everything
Bucks leave their scent at the scrape in two main ways. One way is they urinate or pee in the scrape. The other way is that they leave scent on a branch that is over the scrape. This "licking branch" is chewed and licked and rubbed over the buck's head to leave many smells of the buck.

Scrapes are good to find because bucks come back often to "freshen" the scrapes. (keep them clean of leaves and to leave new scent)

scrape

licking branch

Get out there and look for these clues that deer leave so you can find the deer during deer season. Good Luck!!

Making a Mock Scrape

Scrapes are made by bucks to attract does to his area. He paws the leaves away to leave a clean area of dirt below some tree branches. He urinates or pees in the scrape and rakes his antlers in the branches above the scrape and chews on one of the branches. He also leaves a foot print in the middle of the scrape when he is done making it.

Here is the cool thing. You can make a fake or mock scrape and try to fool the does and other bucks that a another deer made the scrape.

Materials Needed

black marker • foam block • butter or plastic knife • small hand rake
small spray bottle • buck urine • trail camera (optional)

Steps to Making a Mock Scrape:

Step 1 - Making a fake hoof print stamp

• Trace the hoof print on this page onto a piece of paper and cut out the hoof prints.
• Next buy or find a block of foam (the green floral foam in craft stores works good)
• Put the cut out hoof prints on the middle of the foam and trace around them with a black marker.
• After the prints are outlined on the foam, take a butter knife or plastic knife and carefully cut around the prints taking about an inch of foam away from the area around each hoof print. (Have a grown up help you with this!)
• Once this is done, you should have a good hoof print stamp.

FUN TIP: You can also use your stamp to make deer tracks on paper. Dip the stamp in some paint and then press the stamp on a piece of paper.

Step 2 - Making the Scrape

• Find an area being used by the deer. A deer trail or fencerow are good places.
• Pick a spot with some branches hanging down that you can reach.
• Take your small hand rake and clean away all of the leaves, grass and twigs from the area to make a circle about 2 or 3 feet across.
• The area should now just be a circle of dirt below the branches.
• Try to wear rubber boots and keep from touching too much.

Making the scrape

Step 3 - Making it Look and Smell Real

- Take your small rake and rake the branches over the scrape so it looks like a buck raked his antlers through the branches.
- Fill a small spray bottle with buck urine and spray the buck urine in the middle of the scrape. (You may want a grown up help you fill the bottle and spray the scrape. Buck urine has a very strong smell and you do not want to get it on you!)
- The final touch...take the hoof print stamp you made from the foam block and press it into the dirt in the middle of the scrape to make a deer hoof print.

spraying scent in and around the scrape

putting the hoof print in the scrape

here is what it should look like

You have just made a mock scrape. Come back in a few days and see if there are real hoof prints in your scrape. You may also want to spray more buck urine in the scrape to "freshen" the scrape just like a real buck would.

Try making more mock scrapes in the area and see if the deer start to use them. Bucks start making a few real scrapes in late September but make most of them in October in the northern part of the U.S.. Bucks begin making scrapes later in the southern U.S.. Depending on where you live, begin making mock scrapes just before bucks start making their real scrapes. By doing this, you can get the deer visiting your scrapes. If the mock scrape is a good one, the deer may make your scrape their own.

Take pictures of your mock scrapes!!

You can take a picture of the scrape and compare your pictures to real scrapes you find in the woods. You could also place a trail camera next to your scrape and even get pictures of deer visiting your scrape.

47

Shed Antler Hunting...
Family Fun!

Coltin and Cody have fun each year hunting shed antlers with their dad. The two brothers have been going antler hunting with their dad since they were old enough to tag along. Their dad, Marlin, has been shed antler hunting for close to twenty years. He collects not only the whitetail shed antlers he finds but other antlers as well like elk and moose.

Coltin and Cody join their dad each year in the late winter and early spring to hunt for antlers on their farms in Ohio and Indiana. Although the boys haven't found as many as their dad, they have started their own collection of the antlers they each have found.

Where do they find all of these antlers?

They look in open fields like picked crop fields and hay fields. They also look along the edges of woods where the bucks enter and leave the fields. Sometimes they find the antlers in the woods. You just need good eyes and a little luck!!

49

The Habitat Connections

Woodland or Forest Habitat

Woodland or forest habitat can be found in many places across the United States. Woodlands are usually made of trees that lose their leaves each year. These trees are called deciduous trees.

Woodlands are home to many animals. Deer, squirrels, opossum, and turkey all live in woodlands.

The woodland provides many kinds of food for the animals that live there. Many of the trees produce nuts that are eaten by many animals.

Oak trees are common in woodlands. They produce acorns that are a favorite food for many woodland creatures.

Get outdoors and explore a woodland this spring. There is probably a forest or woodland in a state park that you can visit.

As you explore the woodland in the spring, look for the beautiful wildflowers that bloom. Be careful that you do not pick the flowers and leave the woodland as you found it. Remember, it is home to many creatures.

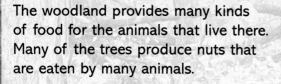

Food Plots

Food Plot-
a small field planted with different plants that birds and animals eat for food.

Types of Food Plots
Annual plots- these are food plots planted with plants that only live for one year. Annual food plots must be planted every year.

Common annual food plot plants include: corn, soybeans, sunflowers, millet, milo, peas and turnips.

Perennial plots- these are food plots planted with plants that grow back every year. Perennial plots do not have to be planted every year. These plots can last for many years.

Common perennial food plot plants include: clover, alfalfa, and chickory

soybeans

clover

Important to Wildlife- Food plots can be very helpful to wildlife. They provide food for birds and animals when there is not much natural food to be found. This can help the birds and animals survive hard times of the year.

Food plots can also provide cover or a place to live and hide for many other animals. Birds and animals that do not even eat the plants sometime make their home in food plots.

Great Tool for Hunters- Food plots are great for attracting game to your land. They are also a good place to set up your stand or blind because the animals visit the food plot often to feed.

Food plots are used all over the country by deer hunters. Deer love feeding on the leaves found in food plots.

Try planting a food plot and see what wildlife you can attract and see!!!

The Muskrat
(Ondatra zibethicus)

Muskrats are a member of the rodent family. They get the name muskrat because of a smelly liquid they secrete. They are found throughout the United States and Canada.

How big are they?

Body - 9-12" long
Tail - 7-12" long
Weight - 1-4 lb.

Muskrat on a log

©istock/Michael Zurawski

Babies, Babies, Babies

Muskrats can have up to four litters of babies each year. Each litter can have 4-7 babies. That's a lot of babies in one year!!

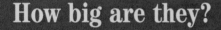

Muskrat lodge

©istock/Lynn Grasing

What habitat do they live in?

Muskrats live in marshes, lakes, ponds, rivers, and streams.

When they live in streams or rivers, they use their sharp claws to dig tunnels into the bank to make their dens.

Muskrats that live in lakes and marshes build lodges. Lodges are large piles of dead plants like cattails or reeds. The muskrat has many different dens inside the lodge. They get into their lodge through underwater tunnels.

52

What do they eat?

Muskrats eat mainly aquatic plants (plants that live in water) like cattails, arrowheads, and duckweeds.

Muskrat carrying food to den

When are they active?

Muskrats are mainly nocturnal, meaning they are most active at night. Sometimes you can see muskrats out swimming in the morning or late evening.

Special Body Parts

Muskrats have adaptations (special parts that help them live better) that allows them to live in their environment.

Sharp claws - these claws help the muskrat to dig tunnels in the bank.

Large webbed, back feet - these help the muskrat to swim well underwater.

Flat tail - the muskrat's flat tail acts like a rudder of a boat to help the muskrat steer itself through the water.

Muskrat slide

Signs to look for:

You can tell muskrats are using an area by looking for signs left behind by the muskrats.

Slides: Slides are muddy areas on the bank where the muskrat slides into the water or goes out of the water. Sometimes you will see claw marks in the mud.

Runs: Runs are like half tunnels under the water. Runs are where muskrats commonly swim as they leave their den or go from one area to another.

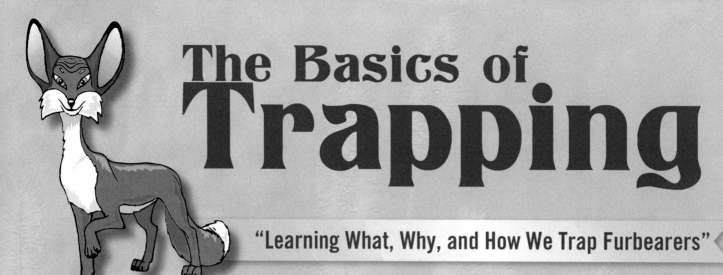

The Basics of Trapping

"Learning What, Why, and How We Trap Furbearers"

What are furbearers?

Although the term **furbearer** includes all animals who have fur, the word usually describes animals that are trapped or hunted for their fur.

bobcat

coyote

What are common furbearers?

Furbearers include animals that live on land and animals that spend much of their time in the water. Here are some examples of common furbearers:

raccoon

Land Furbearers:
- fox
- coyote
- lynx
- marten
- fisher
- bobcat

Water Furbearers:
- beaver
- mink
- nutria
- muskrat
- otter
- raccoon

red fox

river otters

Why do we trap furbearers?

There are many reasons we trap furbearing animals. We will talk about three main reasons.

Reason #1:
We use their fur to make clothing.

People have trapped furbearers for hundreds of years. Native Americans and early explorers used animal skins and furs to make warm clothing.

Today we still use animal fur to make warm fur coats, hats and mittens. The animals' fur is very thick during the winter months (which is when most trapping seasons are open) and this thick fur is very good for insulating against the cold.

Sick fox with mange

Reason #2:
Population Control

Any group of the same animal in an area is called a **population**. If the population becomes too big, animals in that population begin to get too crowded and have a hard time finding enough food to survive. They also get diseases easier.

Trapping allows people to control the populations of animals so that there is not too many animals for an area. This keeps the animals healthy.

Reason #3:
Protect the Environment

If there are too many of one animal in an area, they can hurt the environment. Too many beavers in one area can cause damage to a lot of trees. Muskrats and nutria can also damage the environment if there are too many in an area.

muskrat

Trapping helps to control the numbers of animals in an area so the environment is not hurt.

How do we trap furbearers?

There are many ways to trap furbearers. Trappers use many different kinds of traps. Different traps are used to catch different animals in different places.

Let's learn about some of these different kinds of traps.

Leg-hold Traps

These are traps that are used to catch an animal by its foot or paw. This trap does not harm the animal and the animal can be released unhurt if the trapper does not want to harvest the animal.

Leg-hold traps come in different sizes. Larger traps are used to trap animals such as fox, coyote, raccoons and marten. Small leg-hold traps can be used to catch muskrat and mink.

leghold trap set

Body Gripping or Conibear Traps

These traps are used to catch an animal and quickly and humanely kill the animal when it gets caught. Body gripping traps are usually used in the water.

Body gripping traps also come in different sizes. Large traps are used to catch larger animals like beaver, raccoons and nutria. Smaller traps are used to catch muskrat and mink.

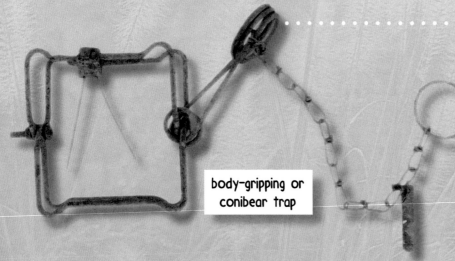

body-gripping or conibear trap

Wire cage Traps

There are two kinds of wire cage traps. One kind is a live trap. These traps are used to catch animals alive so that unwanted animals can be released unharmed.

The other is a wire box trap. This trap is used to catch muskrats and is used underwater in the muskrat runs.

box trap set underwater in a muskrat run

Snares

Snares are made of steel cable that makes a loop that catches the animal. Snares are made so the loop closes on the neck or body of the animal and locks so the loop does not loosen.

Snares are used to catch animals as they walk on a game trail or go in and out of an opening. Snares are used to catch fox, coyote, raccoon and other furbearers.

snare set on a trail

snare

Trapping furbearers is not easy.

The trapper must know the habits of the animals he or she is trying to catch. Knowing where an animal lives, where it travels and how it hunts for food can help the trapper better know where to set the traps to catch that animal.

To become a good trapper, you must learn a lot. The best way to learn is to find someone who has trapped for many years and ask a lot of questions. You can also ask to tag along and watch as the trapper runs his trapline. Learning what traps to use and where to put them are important lessons to learn.

If you ask the right questions and listen to the advice of an experienced trapper, you may some day become an expert trapper yourself. Most states have trapping associations that are groups that can help you learn about trapping. You can also learn more about trapping at the following websites:

www.nationaltrappers.com
www.traps4kids.com/home.html

Red Fox
(Vulpes vulpes)

When someone talks about a fox, the red fox is usually what comes to mind. Red foxes get their name from the color of their fur. No, it is not really red like a firetruck. It is more a rusty, orange color with a white belly.

Where are they found?

Red foxes are one of four types of foxes found in North America. Red foxes did not always live here in the United States. They were brought here from England so people could go fox hunting in this country like they did back in England. The red fox is common in most of the United States and Canada, except for the western part of the U.S..

The red fox's habitat includes woodlands, fields, brushy areas, and pastures.

How big are red foxes?

Their body is about 24 inches long and their bushy tail can be 14-17 inches long. They can weigh between 8 and 15 pounds.

What do they eat?

The red fox is an omnivore, which means it eats meat and plants. Red foxes favorite foods are mice, rats, and rabbits. They do sometimes eat birds, insects and fruits.

Red Foxes are nocturnal, so they are most active at night.

What about red fox babies?

Red fox babies are born in March and April. Red foxes have one litter of 5 or 6 babies called kits. The red fox have their babies in an underground den. The den can be an old groundhog hole or the fox will dig a new den.

Both red fox parents care for the babies. While the mother fox nurses the babies in the den, the father fox will bring food to the den for the mother. Once the babies are eating food, both parents go hunting and bring back mice and other animals for the babies to eat.

The red fox is trapped by trappers for its soft, furry pelt. The red fox is also hunted. Fox hunting with dogs is a tradition in England that goes back hundreds of years.

Foxes can carry disease

If there are too many foxes in an area, they can get diseases. Red foxes can get mange, which is a disease of their skin. Foxes with mange lose their hair and look really nasty. Foxes can also carry rabies, which is a dangerous disease to people.

Never try to touch a fox that looks sick or lets you get close to it!!

Coyote
(Canis latrans)-means Barking Dog

Where they live:

- Almost all of North America, from Mexico to Alaska

- Coyotes first lived in prairies and deserts, but now can be found from the arctic to the tropics.

- They are a member of the dog family and a cousin to the Grey Wolf.

- Coyotes are very intelligent and have a good sense of smell, hearing, and vision.

A coyote's size is between a fox and a wolf.

Average sizes:
Length= 36 inches
Weight= 25-45 pounds
Height= 18 inches (max)
Can run up to 40 mph.
Can jump up to 13 feet.
Live about 8-12 years in the wild

What they look like:

- Pelt is grayish-brown to yellowish gray

- Throat and belly are white to cream in color

- Side of the head, nose, and feet are reddish-brown

- Black stripe down back, with a bushy tail

- Ears are pointed and stand up (this helps to tell the difference between a dog and coyote)

- They have a long nose and 42 teeth.

Coyote parents will give their young pups a live mouse to play with; this teaches them how to become good hunters in the future.

What they eat:

- Omnivore- means they eat meat, plants, and about anything else.

- feed mainly on small mammals like mice, rabbits, prairie dogs, and squirrels.

- will also eat fruits and veggies, sometimes carrion (dead animals).

- In farming areas, coyotes are known to go after baby calves and lambs.

- Coyotes will hunt day and night and sometimes in packs (groups of coyotes).

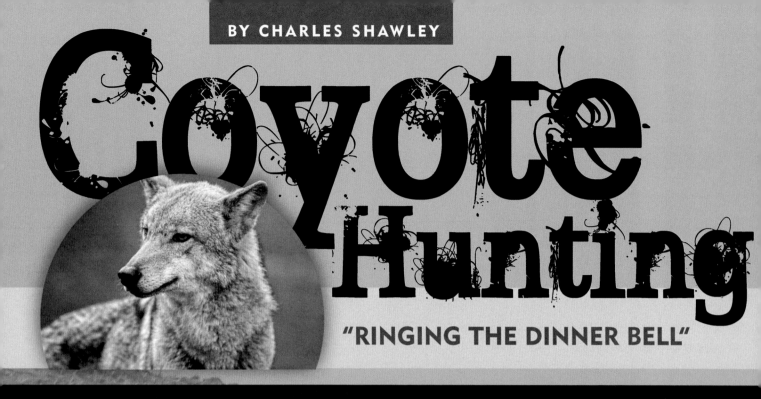

BY CHARLES SHAWLEY

Coyote Hunting

"RINGING THE DINNER BELL"

HUNTING deer and elk is fun, but the seasons are short and they are hard to hunt. Wouldn't it be nice if there was an animal you could hunt all year long and call them right to you. In many states, there is.

The coyote is a canine predator that has to eat 2-3 pounds of food per day to survive. Its normal diet consists of rodents and rabbits, but a coyote will eat just about anything. Farmers and ranchers like coyotes because they eat mice but despise them when they eat valuable produce and livestock. When coyotes do eat calves and lambs, ranchers call coyote hunters.

RING THE BELL

JUST LIKE DEER AND ELK, coyotes can be called. However, coyotes are unique. They can be called to eat just like a ringing dinner bell. A coyote hunter uses an animal distress call to sound like a prey animal that has been injured or captured by a predator. This sound is music to a coyote's ears and tells it that supper is ready. The coyote rushes toward the sound expecting food but instead finds the hunter.

COYOTE CONVERSATION

A COYOTE isn't always hungry. Ringing the dinner bell with a distress call doesn't always interest coyotes. Coyote hunters can also pretend to be a coyote and howl using a howling call, also known as a howler. This tells the coyote that another coyote is in the area. This makes the coyote curious and it may come closer to investigate.

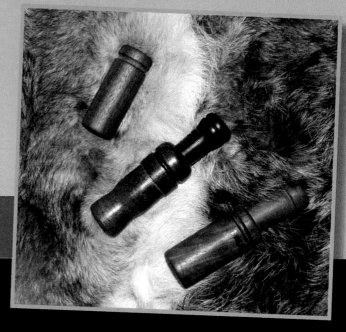

THE CALLS

COYOTE HUNTERS use mouth calls and/or electronic callers. Mouth calls come in several types, and each call will make different types of sound. You simply blow into them just like a kazoo. Diaphragm calls are widely used by turkey hunters but can also be used for coyote hunting to produce almost any sound including coyote howls. Most mouth calls cost $7-$20 and are a great way to get started. All calls require you to practice to really sound good.

ELECTRONIC CALLERS are really cool. The operate like an iPod but instead of headphones there is a speaker. The newer ones are wireless and can be operated by a remote control from a long distance. They are easy to use, make realistic sounds, and can keep a coyote's attention away from where you are sitting, but the good ones are very expensive.

After you have your caller, practice, practice, practice. Mouth calls take some time to master. Listen to other coyote hunters and try to reproduce what you hear. Watch coyote hunting DVD's or TV shows. Study the way those hunters operate their callers. The more you practice, the better you'll sound, and the better you sound, the better your chances of calling a coyote.

FINDING COYOTES

HUNTING COYOTES takes more than just learning to how to call them. You also have to find where they live. Coyotes live where they have food, water, and shelter. Begin by looking at maps for areas that have these three features. Then scout these areas for coyote sign including scat, tracks, dens, and feeding sites. Listen for coyotes howling at dawn and dusk. Talk to neighbors, ranchers, farmers, and the local fish and game department. They can be a great resource for locating areas with coyotes. Have a grown up go with you, and bring a map to mark possible hunting spots.

"COYOTE FEVER"

THE REAL EXCITEMENT of coyote hunting is that you are hunting the hunter. This is very different than hunting deer and elk. Your first several times you may experience what is known as "coyote fever." Coyote fever is not an illness. It is that excitement you feel when calling in a coyote for the first time. Coyote fever will be different for every hunter, but it usually begins with your pulse. Your heart will start to beat fast. Then it affects your eyes. Your focus will be on the coyote and not your aim. In the end, coyote fever may cause you to miss your shot. Don't get frustrated. It happens to the best of us. Practice makes perfect when it comes to coyote hunting. Keep at it, and your coyote fever will pass.

TIPS

HERE ARE SOME TIPS FOR HUNTING COYOTES:

1. Watch the wind. Coyotes have amazing noses and will often circle downwind of you as they approach. If they smell you, they will run away. Sit so that you can watch downwind in case a coyote tries to wind you.

2. Sit with the sun behind you. Make approaching coyotes stare into the sun as they approach. This will help defeat their great vision.

3. Stay in the shade. Try to sit in the shade to hide your movements as you call.

4. Have a grown up help watch behind you. A second set of eyes can be useful for finding coyotes sneaking up from the rear.

5. Be as still as possible. Coyotes see movement very well and any movement will give you away and end the hunt early.

6. Use different sounds. Over time, a coyote may get accustomed to your calls and not be as interested. A new sound may get that coyote excited again.

7. Don't get discouraged. If you are having trouble calling in coyotes, keep at it. Even the best hunters don't call coyotes every time.

HUNTING COYOTES is a great way to keep your hunting skills sharp year round. It is fun, and, at times, the action can be non-stop. There is nothing like hunting the hunter, and once you try it, you'll never want to stop.

Predator Call

The article on coyote hunting talked about calling in coyotes with a distress call. You can of course buy these calls but you can also have fun making one yourself. The "Popsicle Stick Call" makes a soft distress call that will call coyotes, foxes and other predators. Here is how you make one.

Materials you need:

2 popsicle or craft sticks • a small rubber band
a piece of paper • scissors

Step 1

- With your scissors, carefully cut a strip of paper the same width as the sticks.

- The strip of paper should be about 3/4 the length of the stick.

Step 2

- Put the strip of paper all the way to one side of the stick.

- Put the other stick on top of the first stick so the strip of paper is between the two sticks.

Step 3

- Wrap the small rubber band around the end of the stick where the strip of paper was put at the end.

- You may need to wrap the rubber band around the stick many times. You might need a grown up to help you do this.

- Your call is now finished.

Step 4

- Hold the stick at the end where the rubber band is wrapped around the stick.

- Put your lips next to the sticks so you can blow inbetween the sticks.

- Softly blow to make a high pitch sound like a rabbit or mouse squeaking.

Tips:

- You can experiment by blowing harder or softer to make different sounds.

- You may want to ask an experienced caller to let you hear a sound of one of their distress calls and see if you can make your call sound like that one.

- Once you are good at making sounds, go out with a grown up and try to see if you can call in a predator with your special call!!

Good luck!!

ULTIMATE OUTDOOR AND HUNTER SAFETY TIPS

HUNTER SAFETY *Talk*

No matter if you are shooting a BB gun, pellet gun, a rifle, or shotgun, you must always follow the Ten Commandments of Firearm Safety and shoot with a grown up.

#1 Always keep the muzzle pointed in a safe direction.

#2 Don't rely on your gun's "safety". Treat every gun as if it can fire at any time.

#3 Be sure of your target and what's beyond it. Once you pull the trigger you can't stop it.

#4 Always wear eye and ear protection when shooting.

#5 Be sure the barrel is not blocked by mud or any other object before shooting.

#6 If your gun does not fire when the trigger is pulled, HANDLE WITH CARE. Keep the muzzle pointed in a safe direction and get adult help.

#7 Always use the right ammunition for your gun.

#8 Guns should be unloaded when not in use.

#9 Learn how the gun you are using works and how to handle it.

#10 Don't change your gun in any way, and DO have your gun serviced regularly.

Parts of the Gun

To be a safe hunter or shooter, you must know the parts of the guns you shoot and what these parts do. Here is a picture of a pump shotgun and a bolt-action rifle. Study and learn the parts and then have someone quiz you to see if you know all the parts of the guns.

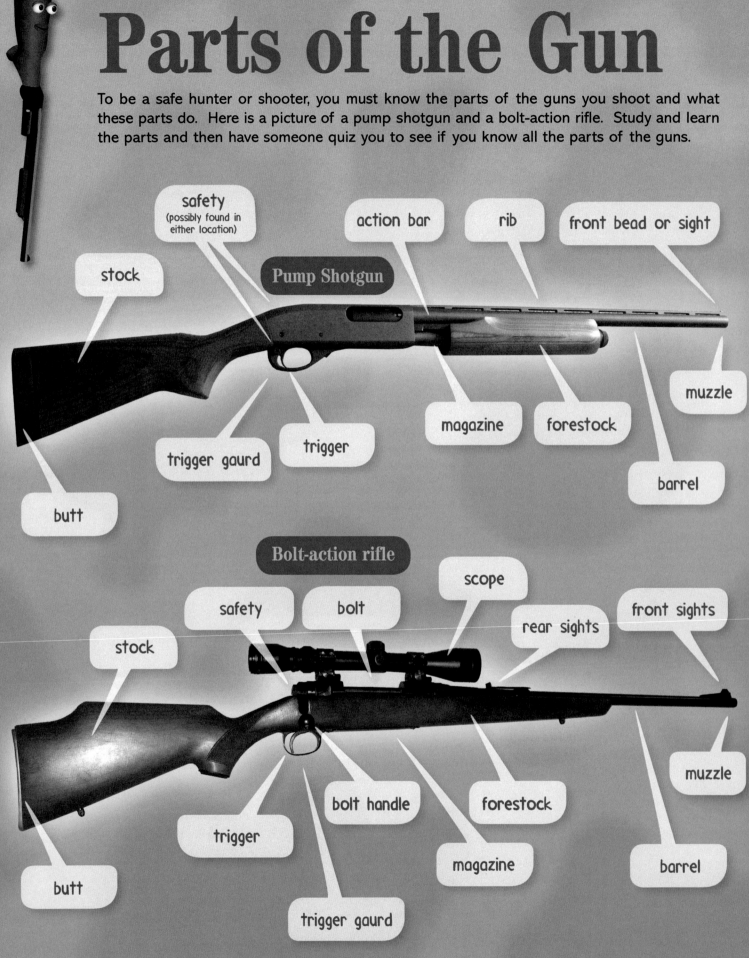

Pump Shotgun

safety (possibly found in either location)

action bar

rib

front bead or sight

stock

muzzle

magazine

forestock

trigger

trigger gaurd

barrel

butt

Bolt-action rifle

scope

safety

bolt

rear sights

front sights

stock

muzzle

bolt handle

forestock

trigger

magazine

barrel

butt

trigger gaurd

Parts of your Archery Tackle

To be a safe hunter or shooter, you must know the parts of the archery equipment you shoot and what these parts do. Here are pictures of some common archery equipment. Study and learn the parts and then have someone quiz you to see if you know all the parts of your equipment.

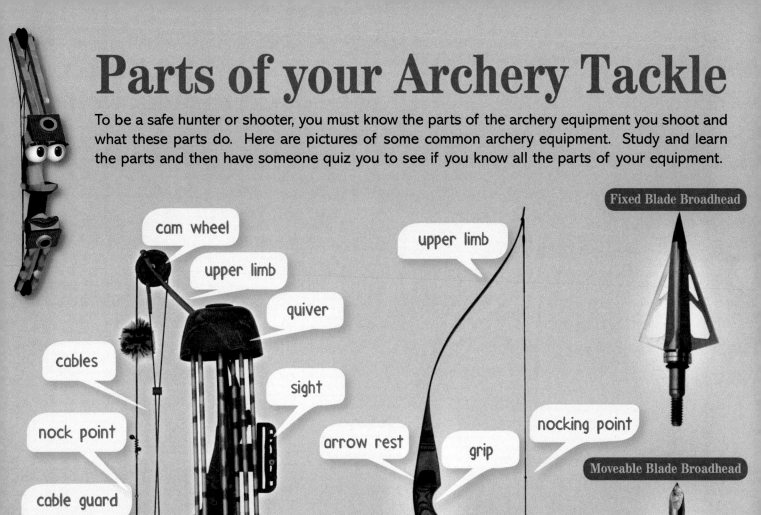

cam wheel

upper limb

quiver

cables

sight

nock point

cable guard

string silencer

lower limb

string

nock

grip

arrows

cock feather

shaft

Compound Bow

upper limb

arrow rest

grip

nocking point

Recurve Bow

string

lower limb

fletching

Arrow

Fixed Blade Broadhead

Moveable Blade Broadhead

Field/Practice Point

Action Types of Rifles

What is the action of a gun? The **action** is the part that loads, fires and unloads the gun. To be a safe hunter, you should know how the different action types of rifles work. The action can be **open** or **closed**. When the action is open, you can see if the gun is loaded or not. If the action is closed, you cannot tell if the gun is loaded. Guns should always be carried and stored with the action open if possible.

Here are the five types of rifle actions. The pictures show the action open and closed.

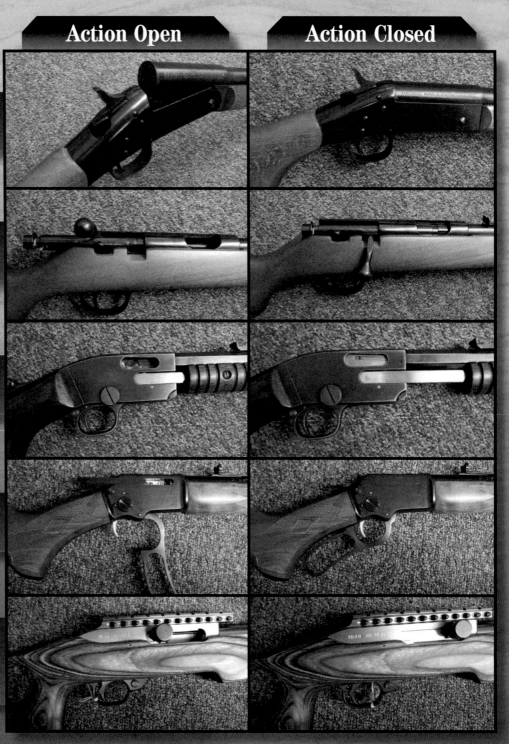

	Action Open	Action Closed
Hinge Action		
Bolt Action		
Pump Action		
Lever Action		
Semi-automatic Action		

What is the Gauge of a Shotgun?

You may have heard someone talking about a 20 gauge shotgun or 12 gauge shotgun. So what is the gauge of a shotgun about? What does the number of the gauge mean?

How a Gauge is Measured

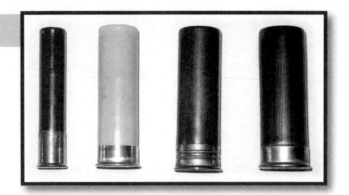

Shotgun gauges are determined by the number of lead balls of a certain size or diameter that are needed to make one pound of that size ball.

This means 12 balls of 12 gauge diameter are needed to make one pound of that size balls, or 20 balls of 20 gauge diameter to make one pound of that size.

The size or diameter of the barrel or bore of the shotgun is not very different for many of the gauges.

For example:

10 gauge = 0.775 inch	16 gauge = 0.662 inch
12 gauge = 0.729 inch	20 gauge = 0.615 inch

The diameter of these are very close to one half to three fourths of an inch.

The Exception

The .410 is named for its bore size, and is not a gauge at all. This means the .410 has a bore or barrel size of 0.410 inch.

The gauge of the shotgun shell is always imprinted in the brass on the end of the shell. If you are not sure what gauge the shell is, look for the number on brass end of the shell.

Safety Note:

ALWAYS BE SURE THAT THE GAUGE OF SHELL MATCHES THE GAUGE OF THE SHOTGUN. A 20 GAUGE SHELL CAN FIT IN A 12 GAUGE SHOTGUN AND BLOCK THE BARREL. IF THE SHOTGUN IS LOADED WITH A 12 GAUGE SHELL AND THEN FIRED, THE GUN MAY BACKFIRE INTO THE SHOOTER'S FACE!! NEVER TOUCH A FIREARM WITHOUT A GROWN UP!

Carry That Gun Safely!!

Whenever you are in the field hunting or going to and from the range to practice, you should always be sure you carry your gun safely. There are six safe ways to carry your gun in different situations. Whenever you carry a gun, you MUST know where the barrel of the gun is always pointing. This is called "**muzzle awareness**".

Two handed or Field Carry

This is good to use when you need to be ready to shoot. It is also good for muzzle awareness in the field.

Cradle Carry

This is a good resting carry. It protects the gun and allows good muzzle awareness in the field. IT SHOULD NOT BE USED IF THERE ARE PEOPLE BESIDE YOU!

Sling Carry

This is a good resting carry when you have to walk a long way. NEVER CROSS A FENCE OR OTHER OBSTACLE USING A SLING CARRY!

Elbow Carry

This is a good resting carry and allows good muzzle awareness. It is good when there are people at your side.

Shoulder Carry

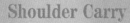

This can be used as a ready carry or resting carry. IT SHOULD NOT BE USED WHEN THERE ARE PEOPLE BEHIND YOU!

Trail Carry

This is the least ready carry. THIS CARRY SHOULD NEVER BE USED WHEN YOU ARE WALKING BEHIND SOMEONE!

*SAFETY NOTE: Always be sure a grown up is with you when you use any firearm.

Basic Shooting Positions

Whenever you shoot a rifle, you must be sure you have a good, steady aim. There are four basic shooting positions you can use when you aim and shoot a rifle. Some of the positions are better than others.

Prone Position

This is the most steady position you can use when you shoot. This position is best because the shooter lays on the ground and cannot move much.

Sitting Position

The next best position is the sitting position. In this position, the shooter sits with both knees up and rests both elbows on the knees to steady the gun.

Kneeling Position

The kneeling position is not as steady as the sitting position because the shooter only rests one elbow on one knee as the shooter kneels down.

Standing or Offhand Position

This position is the least steady of all. If you have to stand while aiming, try to lean up against a tree or a fencepost to help steady the gun.

Safety Note: Remember, only shoot firearms when an adult is with you. Always treat every firearm like it is loaded and always point the muzzle in a safe direction.

Try these different shooting positions but most of all, be SAFE and shoot with a grown up!

POISON IVY
LEAVES OF THREE, LET IT BE

Aren't there 2 types of poison ivy?

Technically there is the climbing variety (toxi-codendron radicans) and the nonclimbing (toxicodendron rydbergii) or Rydberg's poison ivy. But since they interbreed, look very similar, sometimes grow in the same places, and give you the same rash, they are pretty much the same.

Where does it grow?

Everywhere in the US and southern Canada except the far west, deserts and at high altitudes. In the west they have poison oak, which is very similar. Both love roadsides and edges of fields.

How do you get poison ivy?

From touching it, or touching something that has touched it, like your clothes or your dog. You normally get it from touching the leaves, but yanking the vine out by the roots - even in winter - will give you a wicked rash.

And there are more unusual ways to get it, like breathing smoke from firewood burning with poison ivy on it. Which can also put people into the hospital.

What it is like to get it?

At first you get a slight itchy spot, which gets worse and worse. It can be a small itchy area that will annoy you, or it can cover your whole body with giant red sores that will drive you nuts.

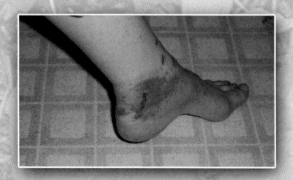

What causes the rash?

There is an oil, called urushiol, that causes an allergic reaction after the first sensitizing exposure. The oil is in the leaves, vines, and roots. That's why tearing out the vine is so dangerous - it releases lot of urushiol.

How long does the rash last?

Anywhere from a week to 3 weeks, depending on how bad it is and how you treat it. Prescription remedies make it go away much faster.

What can you do once the itching starts?

For a serious case you MUST SEE A DOCTOR. For less serious cases check with your local drugstore or see the list below for remedies.

Here are a list of popular home remedies:

• Take a shower in the hottest water you can stand, for as long as you can stand - this should ease the itch for 8 hours.

• Jewelweed is widely thought to help the rash. Mash the weed and apply to the rash.

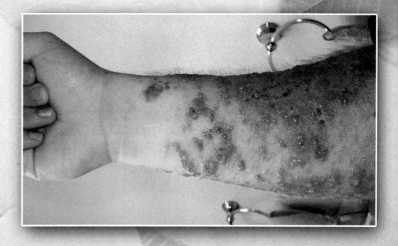

What's good about Poison Ivy?

Poison ivy does have its good points:

• It feeds wild birds and animals who eat its berries without ill effects.
• It holds the earth very well against erosion near the ocean.
• Native Americans had medical uses for it.

And we probably don't know enough about it to know what is it's true value for nature or for man.

The information for this article was taken from Jon Sachs web site, www.poison-ivy.org. This is a wonderful site to learn more about poison ivy.

MOSQUITOES

AVOID THE BITE

istockphoto© Douglas Allen

Mosquitoes are a common pest in the summer. Soon as the sun begins to set, these bugs become a camper's or angler's worst nightmare. Their buzzing and biting can drive you crazy if you do not protect yourself.

Why do mosquitoes bite?

Many people do not know that only the female mosquito bites. Mosquitoes feed on flower nectar but the female mosquitoes need a meal of blood for the eggs developing in their bodies.

The female mosquito will fill up on blood if she is not disturbed during her meal. Once she is done feeding she will fly away (as long as she is not too heavy to fly) and find a place to lay her eggs.

Where do mosquitoes like to live?

Mosquitoes must lay their eggs in water. They like places where the water is still and quiet. Standing water in swamps or forest are good for mosquitoes. Old tires or containers that hold water are also good places for mosquitoes to lay their eggs.

Once the eggs hatch, the baby mosquitoes or larva live under water but come to the surface to breathe. After 4-7 days they become an adult and leave the water to find something or someone to bite.

Baby mosquitoes (larva) underwater

istockphoto©Nancy Nehring

How do they find us?

Mosquitoes find us or other animals they want to bite by three ways. They use sight and look for something to bite. They also can sense the heat coming from us or animals. The last way is they sense the CO_2 or carbon dioxide that we and other animals breath out.

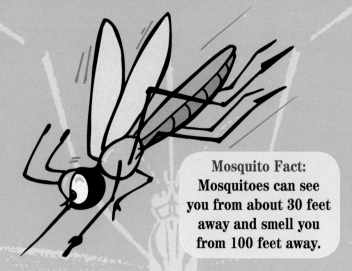

istockphoto©Sebastian Iovannitzi

Mosquito Fact: Mosquitoes can see you from about 30 feet away and smell you from 100 feet away.

Why you don't want to get bit!

When mosquitoes bite, their sharp mouth part called a proboscis goes into your skin. As they bite and suck your blood, their saliva or spit gets into your skin and causes an allergic reaction. This reaction causes a red, itchy bump we call a mosquito bite.

Besides the itchy bites, another reason you do not want to get bit is that some mosquitoes can carry diseases like malaria, encephalitis and the West Nile virus. Although not common, mosquitoes in the United States can carry encephalitis and the West Nile virus.

Mosquito Fact: Mosquitoes like to bite children more than adults.

How do you protect yourself?

There are several ways you can protect yourself from those biting, blood thirsty mosquitoes. The best way is to avoid being out at dusk or dawn when mosquitoes are more active. If you have to go out at those times, you can do a few things to protect yourself.

1. Use a child-friendly insect repellent. These are repellents with 30% DEET or less. It is also important to wash off the spray with soap and water when you get finished being outdoors.

2. Where protective clothing like long sleeves and pants, head nets and/or mesh jackets.

If you avoid the places where mosquitoes like to live and protect yourself, you can still enjoy the outdoors this summer. Just try to avoid the bite!!!

BUG REPELLENT

TICK
CHECK!

Ticks are small creatures related to spiders. They are arachnids not insects. In the spring ticks climb onto grass and twigs waiting for an animal or person to come along.

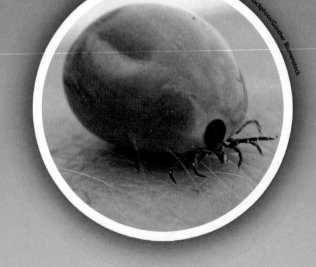

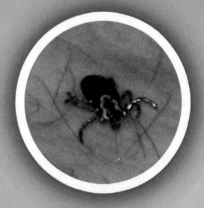

Ticks eat by biting and sucking the blood of an animal or person. They begin very small but grow very large when they fill with blood.

Helpful Tick Tips:

• Use a kid-friendly insect repellent (10% DEET or less) if you are going to be in the woods or tall grass in the springtime.
• Wear light colored clothing so you can see ticks easily.
• Check for ticks soon after returning from the woods or field and remove any ticks as soon as possible.

Although ticks can carry diseases like Lyme's disease, you can protect yourself by following these helpful tips.

You can keep ticks away from you by using repellent on your clothes and skin. Permanone is a spray you put only on your clothes to keep ticks off your clothing. Insect spray with deet is put on the skin to keep ticks away from your skin.

If you find a tick, have an adult remove it by using tweezers and grasping its head near the skin where it is attached. Be sure to get the head and not just the body. It is very easy to pull off the body from the head!

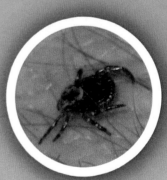

Outdoor Youth Opportunties and Programs

There are many organizations that offer wonderful programs and opportunities for young people to experience and learn more about hunting skills and the outdoors in fun and hands on ways. Here are a few that are offered across the nation that you may be able to find and attend close to where you live.

Trailblazer Adventure Program

 The Trailblazer Adventure program is offered at locations across the nation by the United States Sportsman's Alliance Foundation (USSAF). The program is the largest youth outdoor sports introduction program in America. This one-day program serves as an all-around introduction to the thrill of outdoor sports and the importance of conservation. It is typically hosted at a Boy Scout camp or similar facility. The Trailblazer Adventure Day features a variety of activities, demonstrations and orientation sessions designed to show children and their parents what the outdoor lifestyle is all about. Activities include firearm safety, archery, trapping, fishing and much more. All activities are conducted under the supervision of experienced Trail Guides with an emphasis on safety. Find out more at http://ussportsmen.org/page.aspx?pid=261

NWTF JAKES & Xtreme JAKES Programs

 The JAKES program is offered by the National Wild Turkey Federation. JAKES, which stands for Juniors Acquiring Knowledge, Ethics and Sportsmanship, is open to youth ages 13 and younger. The pro-

 gram teaches youth how to fish, canoe, shoot bows and BB guns, camp and about other general outdoor activities. The NWTF's Xtreme JAKES (ages 13-17) program provides opportunities and challenges more in line with older JAKES abilities and experiences.

 The National Wild Turkey Federation started the JAKES program as a way to give kids the chance to explore their outdoor world through hundreds of fun kids-only events held across North America called JAKES Conservation Field Days. During these events, JAKES members learn cool skills they can take to the field to stay safe and have fun. You can find JAKES events by visiting www.nwtf.org or by calling 1-800-THE-NWTF.

M.U.L.E.Y Program

 The Mule Deer Foundation (MDF) has developed a wonderful youth program called the M.U.L.E.Y (Mindful, Understanding, Legal, Ethical Youth) program. The program's main focus is the safe introduction of youth into the shooting sports and educating youth on the importance of wildlife conservation. At M.U.L.E.Y events youth will have the oppor-

tunity to learn the proper handling, aiming, and firing of rifles, shotguns, handguns, and bows.. Youth will also learn how hunting and wildlife conservation work together by learning the fundamentals of how, when, where, and why to hunt. Youth will also be taught the basic needs of wildlife by focusing on the needs and habitat of the mule deer and black-tailed deer. You can learn more about the M.U.L.E.Y program and how to find a program near you by visiting http://www.mule-deer.org.

4-H Shooting Sports

 The National 4-H Shooting Sports helps to organize state and national shooting events where young people can demonstrate the skills they master from their local clubs. Local 4-H Shooting Sports clubs are open to all youth ages 8 to 18. 4-H is an outreach program conducted through each State Land Grant University. Each year, 4-H teaches a shooting sport to more than 200,000 boys and girls. Shooting sports can be gratifying for youngsters, especially those who aren't athletes. The program provides a supportive environment in which young people can experience hands- on, fun, learning experiences. Explore what you can do with 4-H Shooting Sports at http://www.4-hshootingsports.org.

Pheasants Forever & Quails Forever

Pheasants Forever's (PF) Ringnecks & Quail Forever's (QF) Whistlers programs are part of PF & QF's No Child Left Indoors® (NCLI) initiative. NCLI is dedicated to working with members, chapters and conservation partners to provide opportunities for youth and their families to share our outdoor traditions and develop a conservation ethic. Youth Mentored Hunts, Family Field Days, Shooting Sports Events and Fishing Clinics are just a few of the activities PF & QF Chapters are offering around the country. If you'd like to find a chapter near you, visit our web sites at www.pheasantsforever. com or www.quailforever.com and visit the chapter locator. Then give your local chapter a call to find out when they are holding the next outdoor adventure!.

National Archery in the Schools Program

The National Archery in the Schools Program (NASP) is a program that has been developed to be implemented into schools across the nation and world. The NASP program is designed to teach International style target archery in physical education class 4th-12th grades, core content covers archery history, safety, technique, equipment, mental concentration, core strengthening physical fitness and self-improvement. Students shoot at 80 cm bulls-eye targets placed before an arrow curtain in their gymnasium. Equipment used is state-of-the art and designed to fit every student.

Schools participating in NASP can shoot in several state tournaments and then qualify for the National Shoot held in Louisville, KY and even the World Tournament held in Orlando, FL.

You can find out more about NASP by visiting their website http://nasparchery.com.

National Rifle Association

The National Rifle Association (NRA) has several programs that young people at any age can participate in. Their Eddie Eagle GunSafe program teaches gun safety to Pre-K to third graders. The Youth Hunter Education Challenge (YHEC) is NRA's advanced program in outdoor skills and safety training for young hunters. Open only to those who have completed hunter-safety training at the state or provincial level, the program is conducted under simulated hunting conditions to provide the best practical environment for reinforcing and testing a young hunter's skills. To find out what the NRA has to offer you, go to http://www.nrahq.org/youth/.

Other Organizations that Promote Educating Young People in the Outdoors

There are many other organizations that provide educational magazines and programs that help keep children excited about hunting and wildlife conservation. Although these programs and resources are not hands on, they still provide wonderful ways young people can learn more about hunting and the outdoors.

Whitetails Unlimited

Whitetails Unlimited has several unique programs that promote young people's interest in hunting and the shooting sports.

Whitetails Unlimited's My First Deer Program and Kids on Target programs allow young people to submit materials to be recognized. To find out more about these programs visit http://www.whitetailsunlimited.com.

Safari Club International (SCI)

SCI has created materials that teachers can use in the classroom to teach about wildlife conservation. SCI also has local chapters across the United States that offer programs for young people. You may want to find

an SCI chapter near you and see what they offer. You can find out more about SCI at http://www. scifirstforhunters.org/

Ducks Unlimited (DU)

Ducks Unlimited offer a junior membership for young people 17 and under. This membership allows you to receive the Puddler Online magazine or Ducks Unlimited magazine depending on your age. Find out more at http://www.greenwing.org.

INDEX

Made in the USA
Middletown, DE
07 June 2021

41373264R00049